OIL SPILLS

Also by Madelyn Klein Anderson

ARTHRITIS

ENVIRONMENTAL DISEASES

NEW ZOOS

OIL SPILLS

BY MADELYN KLEIN ANDERSON

FRANKLIN WATTS • A FIRST BOOK
NEW YORK • LONDON • TORONTO • SYDNEY • 1990

Cover photograph courtesy of Picture Group/Al Grillo

Photographs courtesy of: UPI/Bettmann Newsphotos: p. 6;
Carl Glassman: p. 11; U.S. Coast Guard: pp. 12
(Neil D. Ruenzel), 25, 31, 35 bottom, 36, 39, 42, 43,
44, 54; U. S. EPA: pp. 14, 16, 32; American Petroleum
Institute: pp. 29, 34, 40, 51, 53, 56; U.S. Department
of Energy: pp. 35 top, 37, 52.

Library of Congress Cataloging-in-Publication Data

Anderson, Madelyn Klein.
Oil spills / by Madelyn Klein Anderson.
p.   cm.—(A First book)
Includes bibliographical references.
Summary: Describes the problem of oil spills, their effect on the
environment, and what must be done to clean up after them.
ISBN 0-531-10872-4
1. Oil spills—Environmental aspects—Juvenile literature.
2. Pollution—Juvenile literature. [1. Oil spills—Environmental
aspects. 2. Pollution.] I. Title. II. Series.
TD196.P4A54   1990
363.73'82—dc20
90-32896 CIP AC

CONTENTS

TANKERS, WELLS, BICYCLES, AND RAIN

• The ship is one of the largest in the world, the supertanker *Exxon Valdez*. She moves gracefully through the water, her cargo of millions of gallons of oil keeping her steady and low in the water. Too low. She is sailing close to the shore and its dangerous **reefs,** those rocky ridges that rise from the seafloor like mountains. She needs deeper waters, but a ship this size takes miles and several minutes to change course. There is no time. Suddenly, an awful sound of grinding metal fills the air as the reef catches her **hull,** her body, and tears it open. The ship's cargo spills into Prince William Sound, Alaska, and moves onto the shoreline in the largest oil spill yet known in United States waters.

Oil from the stricken tanker *Exxon Valdez* (left) is pumped aboard the *Exxon Baton Rouge* as cleanup efforts on the oil spill take place in Prince William Sound, Alaska

7

The *Torrey Canyon* aground on Pollard Rock in the Scilly Isles. Parts of the rock show at the bottom of the picture.

• Another tanker, another time, another place. This is the *Torrey Canyon,* one of the first supertankers, much smaller than those of today, and this is the north Atlantic Ocean, halfway around the world from Alaska. The ship's captain is anxious to make the high tide that he needs to sail into port, or he will have to wait over for the next tide. Waiting means losing thousands of dollars—ships must move cargo to make money. The captain charts a course that will save time but will bring the ship close to a group of dangerous rocky islands. He looks up to see that he has made an error in his charting and shouts a command to the seaman steering the ship to correct the course. The seaman does not understand the captain's orders and steers onto the rocks instead. Oil from the wrecked *Torrey Canyon* spills into the Atlantic Ocean for weeks and washes up onto the coasts of Great Britain, France, Holland, Belgium, and Spain. The world watches, and for the first time recognizes the threat of oil spills to the environment. People take steps to keep these disasters from happening again, but they do.

• Another giant spill, several years later, in Campeche Bay in the Gulf of Mexico. This spill is not from a tanker, but from a well that has been dug under the sea to meet the great demand for oil. A drill breaks through the rocks covering a bed of oil that has been sealed for many centuries. Released from the pressure it has been under, the oil shoots high into the air, and there is no drilling mud to hold it back. Someone forgot to order the mud. It takes almost two years to put a cap on the well to get it under control. This spill from the well known as Ixtoc I is the largest oil spill in history—so far.

Accidents such as these spill about 100,000 tons of oil every year, according to statistics from the National Academy of Sciences. These kinds of accidents can do a lot of harm to the environment when they reach shorelines, and they receive a lot of publicity. But oil is spilled in greater amounts in other ways, ways that do not get into newspapers or on television. The National Academy of Sciences estimates that 2 million tons of oil enter the ocean every year from the routine transportation of oil, twenty times more than comes from accidents. Oil is always being moved, from the time it comes from a well and through a pipeline. Supertankers may carry the oil across oceans, but there are very few ports deep enough for them to dock. So oil has to be moved into smaller tankers that can make port, then into barges and storage tanks. Oil is usually delivered to **refineries**—places where oil is changed into its many different forms—and moved again in pipelines, ships, railway cars, and tank trucks. Along the way, loading and unloading may be careless, pipelines may crack, hose connections may break, tanks may leak, and hundreds of other things may happen to cause oil to spill.

Many more thousands of tons of oil are spilled deliberately. About half of the world's merchant ships, and almost all small pleasure boats, use the sea as a

Tugs move barges like this up and down rivers, bringing petroleum products where tankers cannot go.

This tug has temporarily lost control of its gasoline barge in choppy water and a tricky current. Fortunately, river traffic is not heavy, so there is no danger of collision with another vessel.

big dumping ground, emptying oily waste water from the bottoms of holds. Tankers also clean their tanks between cargoes, flushing out tarry old oil from their walls. They empty oil in their **ballast,** water used to fill the tanks when there is no cargo so that the ship does not roll. Cleaning out tanks and emptying the ballast at sea are against the law. Collection stations are provided to receive these oily waters, but many ships do not want to spend the time to use them.

Many of the spills are too small to do much harm to the environment, but others are quite harmful. Wasting such great amounts of oil every year is dangerous. Oil is not replaceable in large amounts, and it is possible that the world will run out of oil one day.

Still more oil is spilled in ways you might find hard to believe.

The National Academy of Sciences estimates that about 1.5 million tons of oil are spilled by you and me and millions of others like us. We oil the gears of our bicycles, change the oil in our cars, and spill the old oil down a drain. A little gasoline (an oil product) drips when a tank is being filled, vehicles leak oil from faulty engines—millions of little spills that add up to a million and a half tons a year. How does this oil reach the sea? It gets flushed into sewers by rain and snow and by sanitation department

Transferring oil cargo can often be a cause of spills.

Dumping old oil taken from the engine of a car. In the
United States alone, almost half a billion gallons of this
kind of used oil enter groundwater through land dumping or
enter the sea through sewers and sewage-treatment plants.
Some areas have collection centers for drained oil and send it
away for re-refining. If there isn't a collection center in your
neighborhood, you may want to look into starting one yourself.

Somebody has carelessly left a hose to drip oil into the ground, where it will reach groundwater.

trucks and by people using hoses. Sewers also have an outlet somewhere in waterways.

And, believe it or not, oil also spills from the sky.

Yes. The National Academy of Sciences tells us that over 600,000 tons of oil a year fall with rain and snow into our oceans. Of course, the oil doesn't pour down, but falls gently as a vapor or mist. Oil is petroleum, a collection of many **hydrocarbons,** chemical compounds or combinations of hydrogen and carbon, and a few other chemicals. When petroleum hydrocarbons are made into fuels and burned, in automobile engines or factories, the smoke or exhaust carries hydrocarbons into the air, into clouds. Wind and air currents usually carry the clouds over oceans, where the hydrocarbons fall with the rain and snow.

Six million tons of oil are spilled every year. What does this mean to us, what does oil—petroleum—mean to us?

Lots of cars mean lots of engines burning fuel, sending lots of petroleum hydrocarbons into the sky, where they will fall to the ground in rain and snow.

2 PRECIOUS PETROLEUM

Plant and animal life that has been buried under water, earth, and rocks for thousands of years changes into hydrocarbons of coal, natural gas, or petroleum, depending on where they were buried and how the hydrocarbons combined.

Petroleum is found in rocks in the Earth's crust in three forms. One form is *crude oil*—a liquid that may be black, brown, green, or even colorless. Another is *asphalt*—a very thick, almost solid, form. A third petroleum form is *natural gas*. This is a science puzzler, since natural gas also forms separately, with its own hydrocarbon structure.

Human beings have known about petroleum since very early times. Small amounts were scooped up from shallow pools and pits. The ancient Chinese used long bamboo tubes to draw it up from the ground.

The petroleum was used by the Chinese for water-proofing their homes and boats and as firebombs in war. The Babylonians paved their streets with petroleum, and the ancient Egyptians used it to grease the axles of their chariots. The ancient Persians took petroleum as medicine, particularly in the asphalt form. When they conquered Egypt in 525 B.C., the Persians broke up the mummies they found, thinking they were covered in asphalt, and ate them. In modern times, around 1815, the city of Prague, in what is now Czechoslovakia, lit streets with petroleum lamps. Native Americans used petroleum for making magic and for paints and medicines. American settlers moving west on wagon trains learned about the native medicines and eagerly traded for them. Soon peddlers bottled them and sold them as snake oil or Genesee oil or Seneca oil—"Good for everything that ails you and your horse and wagon, too!"

Then, in 1859 in a little town in Pennsylvania, now called Titusville, a well was dug to bring oil out of the ground like water. That well changed the world.

Once oil could be brought up from the ground in large quantities, ways were found to use it. This meant changing petroleum's form. Like all liquids, petroleum can be boiled. You have seen water boiling in a pot or kettle giving off steam or vapor. When pe-

The first oil well. The man in the top hat is Edwin Drake, the developer.

troleum is boiled, the vapor it lets off can be collected and turned into different forms called **fractions,** leaving behind **residual oils** that are refined in other ways. Different fractions result from boiling petroleum at different temperatures. All petroleums produce the fractions kerosene, naphtha, benzene, and gasoline. Particular petroleums also produce heavier fractions such as fuel oils, lubricating oils, medicinal oils—including the familiar mineral oil and petrolatum (we know petrolatum as petroleum jelly or by its trademark name Vaseline)—and paraffin. Pennsylvania petroleums are particularly rich in paraffin.

At first, the fractions most often used were paraffin for candles and kerosene for lamps. Gasoline was tried as a fuel for use in stoves and lighting lamps, but it exploded. Gasoline was considered unusable, and most of it was dumped. But a few people experimented with it, and it was the existence of gasoline as a fuel that made possible the invention of the automobile and other engine-driven machines.

The demand for gasoline became enormous. Scientists searched for faster ways to produce it and came up with a process called **cracking.** Cracking left behind new kinds of residual oils. These were soon turned into many now-familiar products, among them alcohol, acetone, ammonia, synthetic rubber, and plastics.

Without petroleum, our world as we know it would come to a stop. The United States uses the most petroleum of any country in the world. Although the United States has great supplies of petroleum, we buy more from other countries. Some of these countries have used our need for petroleum to gain power as well as great wealth. In the middle

1980s, these countries demanded such high prices for their oil that they caused severe economic problems around the world.

Oil spills can mean economic problems on a less global scale as well. Fishermen are deprived of their catches and hotel owners lose guests because of oiled beaches. We all face the possibility of financial hardship from the effects of oil spills. We all suffer, too, from the deaths of birds and fish and other animals that an oil spill can cause.

Oil spill in a marina—it won't be a pleasure to clean the oil from the hulls of these crafts.

3 OIL AND WATER

You can see for yourself the way that oil behaves in water. Fill a small bowl about halfway up with water. Pour in a tablespoon or two of mineral oil, a petroleum product. If you don't have any, use cooking oil, a vegetable product that works in the same way for this experiment. Now watch. Does the oil make a large circle on top of the water? It should, because the oil is lighter than the water, and it is also the nature of oil to cling together in a circle rather than spread out. You have made an **oil slick.** This is how a spill starts out.

Now stir the slick up with a fork, and wait a few minutes. You will see most, but not all, of the slick form again. As you stirred, a little of the oil mixed with the water and dissolved or became heavier and sank below the top. Now leave your oil spill in the sun for a few days if you can. A lot of the slick and the water will **evaporate,** change into a vapor and rise into the air, and you will be left with a kind of goo on the bottom of your bowl. Oil spilled into those great bowls holding the Earth's waters behaves in much the same way as it does in your bowl.

When oil spills into those waters, it first forms a slick. Then **weathering**—the action of sun, wind, waves, rain, and tides—acts like your fork to stir up the oil so that some of it mixes with the water and dissolves or sinks. Meanwhile, the sun evaporates some more of the oil on top of the water. **Bacteria,** microscopic organisms, also **biodegrade,** or break down, the oil. These natural processes clean away half to three-quarters of an oil spill in open water. How much and how quickly the oil breaks down depends on many **variables,** differences in the spill. The type of oil, the kind of water, the temperature and weather, and the place are some of the variables. For instance, a small spill in the icy waters of the Arctic or Antarctic oceans may never disappear, or a spill of heavy oil may take months longer to degrade than a light one.

Oil slicks don't stay put in open water as they do when they are contained in your bowl. They move on the currents and with the tides—toward shore, away from shore, toward shore, away from shore. If everyone is lucky, they never reach shore. But most of the time they do. If you've ever gone bathing in a bay or ocean, you probably got a blackish, oily smear of "tar" on the soles of your feet. That was oil that had weathered for a long time in the sea and had finally reached shore to stain the beaches—and you.

When weathered, tarry oil or heavy crude oil reaches the shore, it does not sink in but stays on top of the ground. This oil does the most damage to small insects and animals such as clams, mussels, and sand crabs who cannot move away from harm quickly enough or who move into the oil without suspecting its dangers. This oil that stays on top of the ground can mat an animal's coat and prevent it from moving quickly to escape its enemies or to hunt prey for food. A bird that comes down on oil gets it on its feathers and down, the fluff that lies between its feathers and skin. When its down is matted by oil, a bird cannot trap the air it needs to help it fly or to keep it warm or cool. Without this means of regulating its temperature, something we humans do inside our bodies automatically, a bird dies. The oil on its feathers can also be taken into the body and poison the bird when it **preens,** uses its beak to clean its feathers and set them in the proper position. Oil on top of the ground also destroys the leaves of plants

Close-up of tar balls washed up on an Arctic beach twenty-eight days after an oil spill

A heavily oiled victim of a spill

that many animals depend on for food. Without those plants, the animals may die.

Light oils sink into the soil. They do more harm to plants than heavy oil because they destroy roots, and then the plants cannot regrow. Light oils that sink are more harmful than heavy oils to animals that **burrow,** dig into the ground to make their homes or escape their enemies. And light oils can also reach **groundwater,** the water lying beneath the surface of the Earth. Groundwater supplies wells and springs, which in turn supply drinking water for animals and human beings.

Oil can affect animals in many other ways. An oiled animal may lose its ability to reproduce. Eggs may not hatch, or offspring may be born deformed. Fish that must reach certain waters to **spawn,** produce its young, may not be able to do so if oil blocks their path.

Oil spills also change the lives of animals in ways that are not easily seen. All animals are linked together by their feeding habits, by what they eat and whether they are eaten. This is called a **food chain.** When large numbers of animals die—in an oil spill, for instance—the animals or vegetables they once ate are no longer eaten, and thrive. But the animals that once ate the now-lost foods have to find other food or die, and the new sources of food now die in greater numbers. Such changes move up and down a food chain and change the pattern of who survives and who does not.

We human beings are at the top of the food chain—we are not hunted and eaten. But we, too, may suffer harm through the food chain. We may eat a fish that has eaten a fish that has eaten a fish that has eaten microscopic plants and animals in the sea called **plankton.** If any of those links has oil in it, the oil will reach us. We may eat meat or drink milk from animals that have eaten vegetation and drunk from springs fed by groundwater containing hydrocarbons. Scientists don't really agree on whether hydrocarbons in our food supply do us harm. They do know that some petroleum fractions, like benzene, are **carcinogens,** cancer-causing agents, in laboratory animals. In what amounts they would cause cancer in human beings is not known, but probably in far greater quantities than are normally taken into the body over a lifetime.

The effects of an oil spill spread like ripples in water when you toss in a pebble. They are felt far away from any spill and in ways we can't always predict or know.

4. CLEANING UP OIL SPILLS

We can do two major things about oil spills: we can try to prevent them, and we can clean them up quickly when they happen. Cleaning up a spill is easiest when it is done as soon as possible after a spill occurs, particularly when it is a spill into water.

Spills of over a gallon of oil are supposed to be reported to the Coast Guard if the spill is into a waterway. The Environmental Protection Agency is to be notified if the spill is on land. If the spiller does not report the spill, heavy fines can be imposed. Most spillers do report, but some do not. The cost of cleanup and the possibility of being sued for damage to the environment can be more than some small or financially troubled companies can pay, and they may try to get away with it. Some tugboats carry cases of dishwashing detergent to pour on small spills to clean them right away so they will not have to report the spills. But not only is it illegal not to report a spill, it is also illegal to use chemicals for cleanup that may do more harm than the oil itself.

In the United States, many teams respond to the alarm of an oil spill. These response teams come from the Coast Guard; the Environmental Protection Agency; state, city, and local environmental protec-

A cleanup team in a practice drill

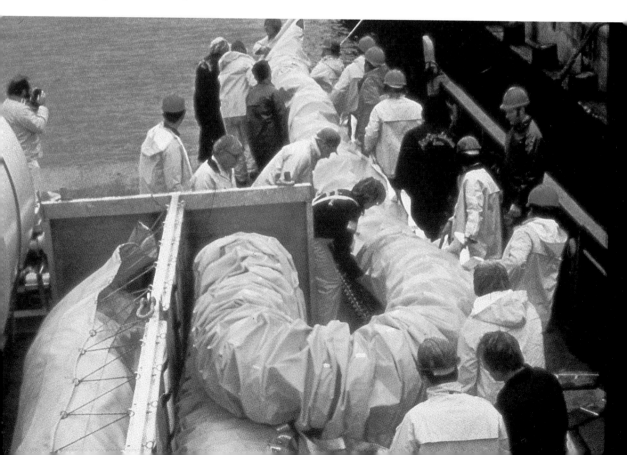

tion agencies; fire departments; private cleanup firms; and usually the large companies that handle petroleum products. These teams may have different ideas on how to go about cleaning up a spill. They each have prepared plans for just such emergencies, but many variables in a spill must be considered on the spot. So the plans provide for a coordinator to be chosen to lead the teams and to make the final decisions on what to do and how to do it. That doesn't mean that everyone is happy with the decisions. For a long time after the *Exxon Valdez* spill, some experts were still arguing that the early use of detergents would have broken up the oil slick faster so that there would have been less damage to the shoreline.

Deciding how to clean an oil spill is not easy. But the first thing that is usually done is to keep the oil from spreading—to contain it.

CONTAINMENT

Think of the cleanup problem you would have if the oil and water in your bowl were to spill on the kitchen table. If you didn't do something quickly, the oil would drip to the floor and spread, and you'd have twice the job to clean it up. Response teams face the same problem.

Laying boom at the *Exxon Valdez* spill in Alaska

To keep an oil spill from spreading, the team may dig a ditch around it if the spill is on land. If it is in water, the team puts up a floating fence called a **boom.** Booms work best in quiet water. If the water is flowing quickly, the boom has to run with it at just the right speed or the oil will escape under it. If there are waves, the oil can wash right over the boom. Nor do booms work on "rainbow spills," spills of oil

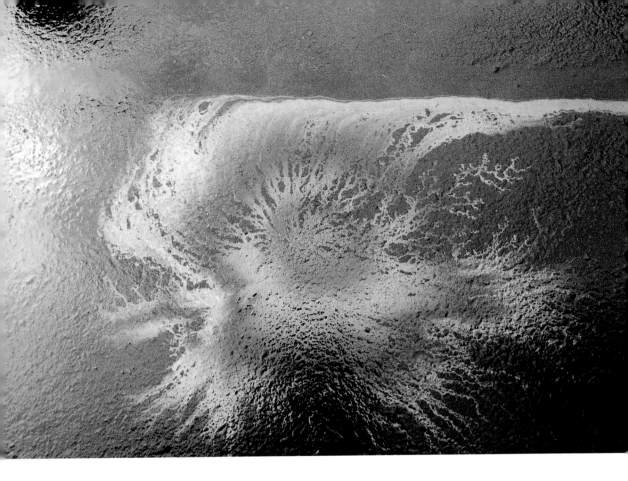

A "rainbow spill"

so thin that they are little more than a sheen on the water. (You can see little "rainbow spills" in puddles on heavily trafficked streets after a rain.)

There are different kinds of booms. Some work like jack-in-the-boxes, popping out and inflating automatically. Some booms come in sections that can be joined to make very long barriers. A boom can also be made of bubbles. Machines that create these bubble barriers are installed in places where there are small but constant leaks into the water, usually at a refinery. One small refinery in New York, for instance, has been leaking ever since it was built, over a hundred years ago. Now a bubble barrier keeps the oil from spreading into the waterways.

Booms are not only used as fences, but also as *herders,* moving oil out of currents or pulling slicks together for easier pickup, like cowboys with lassos herding cattle.

CLEANUP

Once the oil is contained, it can be picked up, chemically acted on by detergents, burned off, or even eaten by special mixes of bacteria.

Skimming—picking up the oil from the top of the water with machines—is a favored cleanup method in the United States. Skimmers may be moved around like huge vacuum cleaners or they can move themselves. Most have storage tanks in them so that the oil and water have a chance to sit quietly until the oil rises to the top, as in your bowl. Then the water can be released from the bottom of the storage tank and the oil saved to be used again. Unfortunately, skimmers do not work well in windy weather that raises waves over two feet high—not very high for a wave—or if the waves are steep rather than

Skimmer, on top. Below it is a storage tank, and to the left, a boom. Boom and skimmer are swung from the side of a vessel, the boom to contain the oil, the skimmer to retrieve it for storage in the tank until it can be taken to a refinery.

sloped. This is because skimmers do not go up and down with the waves but right through them, missing the oil floating on the top.

Pumping is a method used with skimmers, but pumps can also be used by themselves. Huge vacuum pump trucks work on spills close to shore. Pumps at sea pull up oil and release it into the hold of a waiting tanker or into a floating storage unit.

Not a Martian spacecraft, but a pumping system. The oil is picked up by hoses (not shown) that connect with the six inlet openings on the right. The oil is discharged through the three hoses on the left.

Storage-tank truck pumping up oil

Laying down sorbent pads at a small spill near a pier

    Absorbents, or **sorbents** for short, are used like sponges to soak up oil. On land, sorbents may be raked or shoveled into the oil. Sorbent barriers or pads laid down in trenches may protect a beach. When waves break over the trench, the sorbents absorb the oil while the water sinks into the sand. On water, sorbents may be mixed directly into the oil or made into pillows or pads and used like booms to catch the oil. Revolving belts of sorbents may be used on skimmers. Mops of sorbents, called "snares," are

The orange sorbent belt passes down into a wringer that squeezes the oil into a holding tank.

used to pick up spills on ice. Sorbents can be squeezed out so that some of the oil they pick up can be retrieved. The problem then becomes one of getting rid of the oily sorbents, which have to be burned or buried.

Burning is another way to clean up oil spills, but this is safe to do only on open water or snow. Getting the oil to burn is no easy matter. Sometimes bombs are dropped from airplanes to set the fires. It is hard to start the fire burning and harder still to keep it lit. Special materials are used to act as wicks to keep feeding the fire.

Dispersants, a mild form of detergent, are favored as a cleanup method in Great Britain. They have recently been approved for use in the United States by the National Academy of Sciences, but cleanup experts still disagreed on their use in the *Exxon Valdez* spill in 1989. To see how dispersants work on an oil spill, squirt a little dishwashing detergent into your bowl with the oil-water mix. The oil breaks up and darts away. This is one of the reasons why dispersants are not everyone's favorite choice for cleanup: if the oil darts off, it is almost impossible to recover. But now stir the oil, as wind and waves would, and you will see the oil-water-detergent mix break up into thousands of tiny bubbles. Dispersants used on a spill do the same thing,

Burning off an oil spill. This tanker collided with
a freighter in fog. Both ships caught on fire, killing
sixteen people. Many thousands of gallons of foam
had to be used to cool the tanker's hull before cleanup
teams could stand on the decks to close off spill sources.
Then they set fire to the oil in the water to clear it away.

and this makes Mother Nature's disposal job easier and faster. The faster a spill is cleaned up, the less danger there is to shoreline and animal life. This is why other cleanup experts favor dispersants.

Bacteria that eat only oil have been developed but are rarely used. The first patent issued to a life-form created in a laboratory by genetic engineering was for oil-eating bacteria. Fertilizer was used at the *Exxon Valdez* spill cleanup to speed the action of bacteria on oil.

People. Oil that reaches the shore is often a gooey, chocolate-colored-looking mess made three times its original size by water. This inflated, sticky mixture is called **mousse.** Mousse (pronounced moose) is really a delicious pudding, usually chocolate, made fluffy and airy and larger by beating. Oil mousse is certainly not delicious, but otherwise it seems to be a good description. Picture yourself picking up a dessert mousse that spills all over the kitchen. It takes a lot of washing and scraping. And in the end, that is how most oil spills are cleaned up. Hardworking people use hoses and shovels, knives, and rags, and anything else that can get the job done, to clean up a spill inch by inch.

This cleanup vessel works in several ways. The tall water guns on either side stir up a slick so it will biodegrade faster. Two doors in the bow form a V-shaped boom that acts like a funnel, herding the oil into a 10,000-gallon storage tank in the hull.

In the end, it's people who clean up oil
spills bit by bit. Left: Steam hosing is used
to clean rocky beaches in Prince William
Sound, Alaska, after the *Exxon Valdez* spill

**Cleanup efforts in Prince William Sound, Alaska, after
the *Exxon Valdez* spill. Although there were complaints that
not enough was done, the cleanup effort was massive.**

Sometimes the best thing to do in an oil spill is not to clean it up at all, but to let nature take care of it. Hauling cleanup machinery and hundreds of people into fragile environments may do more harm than done by the oil, unless there is a threat to homes, endangered species, or to large numbers of animals in a fish hatchery or bird sanctuary. But it is hard to convince the public of this.

DISPOSAL

What do you do with all that mousse, those tar balls, the oiled sand and plant life and rags and sorbents from a spill cleanup? Disposal can be a problem. Cleanup teams at one spill in Santa Barbara, California, for instance, found they had 10,000 truckloads of oily sorbents to be disposed of.

Waste sorbents and other cleanup materials are usually buried in landfills. Some people believe that this is not a very good solution. The oil seeps and can reach groundwater or farmland if the landfill is not properly designed, and the spill may not allow for careful planning of a landfill. Oiled debris is sometimes spread over the ground and left to rot, and oiled sand and gravel are sometimes used on roads being built. This is called **landspreading.** Although landspreading may cause the same seepage problems as burial, more of the oil evaporates when it is in open air. Oily waste may also be burned, but this causes heavy smoke pollution if it is not carefully controlled in incinerators. It is not only cleaning up spills that is a problem, but cleaning up the cleanup as well!

CLEANING WILDLIFE

Cleaning animals oiled in a spill is a special problem. Most of them are beyond help, but great efforts to save them are made anyway. If the animals can stand being captured, if they are given expert help, and if they are not badly oiled, some will survive.

Caring for an animal that most likely will die is very difficult. If you should find a bird or other animal that has been oiled, do not try to care for it yourself. Anyone who handles animals must have a federal permit. This has been the law for many years and was meant to protect birds from being slaughtered for their feathers in the days when feathered hats were popular. Besides, you are not able to give the animal the care and time it needs to recover. Seabirds especially make quite a mess and have to be tended and fed twenty-four hours a day for weeks on end.

It is best for you and for the animal to get trained

help: a veterinarian, the local zoo, even medical specialists who can give injections and medicines. You can find out where to go from the Coast Guard, the Environmental Protection Agency, the Fish and Wildlife Service, the local wildlife or environmental agency, or the local Audubon Society or Society for the Prevention of Cruelty to Animals. If you live close to a large spill, a care center will be set up there to receive animals, most of which will be birds. These centers are usually staffed by volunteer experts who fly in from all parts of the country. The International Bird Rescue Research Center at Berkeley, California, trains such groups, as does the Audubon Society.

You may even be able to volunteer at the center. You probably won't work directly with the animals, but lots of help is needed to lay down newspapers in pens and cages and to clean and sweep. Or you may be needed to shout and wave and blow horns to scare birds away from landing in oil.

Handling oiled animals requires care, gentleness, and speed. The animals are frightened of people and frightened at what is happening to them. They are likely to scratch and claw and bite. Tranquilizers help. Sometimes a sock with a slit cut in the toe for the beak to poke out seems to calm birds and keep them controlled and warm at the same time. After medical care is given, the animals are cleaned, usually with

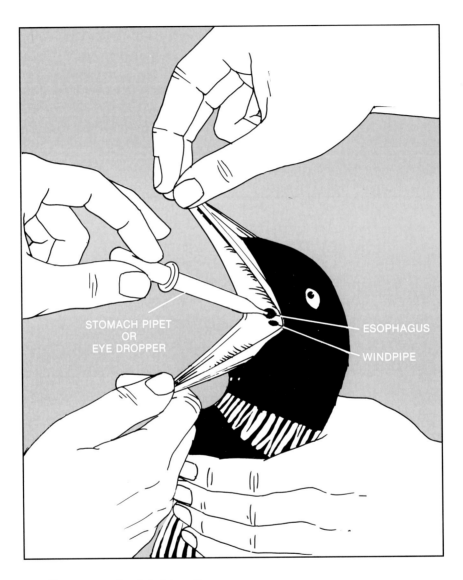

STOMACH PIPET
OR
EYE DROPPER

ESOPHAGUS

WINDPIPE

Feeding a captive bird is often
difficult, as this diagram shows.

detergents. Detergents have to be rubbed in very carefully so as not to damage coats, particularly feathers. A bird's feathers have to be moved and placed only in their one natural direction. Using detergents also requires a lot of rinsing or their skins break out in sores.

Once the animals are cleaned and patted dry with towels or rags, they are left to rest. Then they are fed—no easy matter. Sometimes birds are too upset to eat, and the food has to be put into their throats and gently massaged down. Diets vary according to the types of animals. In a big spill, railroad cars or caravans of refrigerator trucks may have to bring in all the grains, greens, worms, insects, fish, and other foods that the animals need.

Many experts say that handling a wild animal and keeping it in captivity too long will make it unable to survive after it is released. There are those who say that heavily oiled animals should be put quickly and painlessly to death instead of making them go through the ordeal of cleanup, which only a few survive. This would also leave more time to help those with the best chance of survival, the lightly oiled animals.

Wouldn't it be a lot better to prevent oil spills? But preventing oil spills is not an easy matter.

5 PREVENTING OIL SPILLS

Many kinds of laws, rules, and regulations have been passed to prevent oil spills. Most of them were laid down after the wreck of the *Torrey Canyon* made the world aware of the importance of our environment.

No ship or facility handling oil can function, nor can an exploratory oil well be drilled, without a special plan to work out every detail to prevent spills and to clean them if prevention fails. Practice response drills are held like school fire drills so that everyone knows what to do and how to do it when a spill alarm comes in. Quick response and quick reporting of a spill help keep damage down. The Coast Guard and the Environmental Protection Agency encourage everyone—including you—to call immediately to report spills.

The *Argo Merchant,* shown here, is famous in oil spill history. It went aground off Nantucket Island in Massachusetts. The captain claimed the ship was not seaworthy and the equipment so old and bad that he didn't know where he was. This spill led to new laws in the United States that forbade entry to foreign ships unless they have proper navigating equipment and are in good condition.

Prevention—an oil spill sweeper and boom
protect a natural gas drilling rig.

Devices of all sorts have been developed to prevent spills. X-ray machines search the insides of pipelines for cracks, and electronic scanners and sensors detect spills. Alarm systems, automatic shutdown valves, oil rig blowout preventers, and dozens of other aids can also be used. Electronic monitors

Testing equipment for cleaning oil spills at the
Department of Energy test facility, OMSETT, in
New Jersey. Machines can move the water to
imitate conditions in rivers and seas.

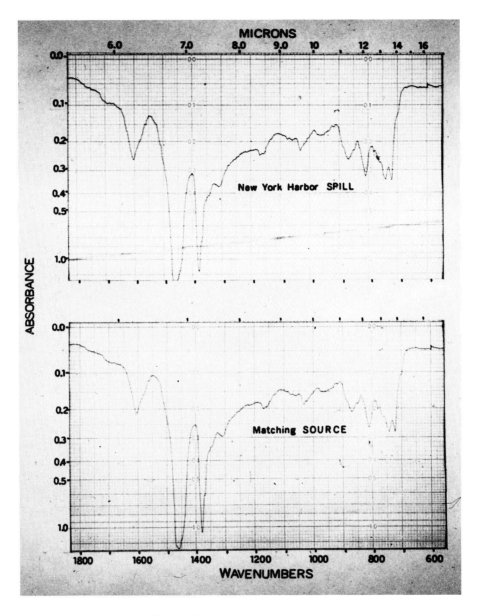

Fingerprinting an oil spill. See how
closely the readings match.

and infrared and other sensors on Coast Guard patrol planes watch for ships that might clean out at sea. Laboratories identify oil from a slick and match it to the ship that spilled it—a process like fingerprinting.

To help prevent future spills, spillers are punished with fines and jail sentences. They may be sued by the government or private agencies for the damage they do to the environment. Companies such as Exxon find themselves boycotted and taken to task in the press and on television and radio. They lose business as well as having to pay for cleanup, damages, and fines. No business wants this to happen to it. Contrary to what many people think, businesses handling oil try very hard to prevent spills.

Companies concerned with handling oil, government agencies, and private schools offer training programs of all kinds to make people aware of what to do and how to do it properly so that oil is not spilled. Representatives of the government check ships, refineries, and storage tanks. They hold safety meetings and post rules and regulations in several languages to educate oil handlers.

Nine out of ten oil spills are caused by people—people doing the wrong things, making mistakes, getting drunk, falling asleep on the job. If people could be trained not to do these things, abracadabra!—almost no oil spills would occur. That *would* take

Simple warning signs to make oil handlers aware of danger

magic. It would be nice to think that everyone could be taught to do everything right all the time. But people do not always do things right. They do get drunk, they do forget, they do make mistakes, they do misunderstand, and they do break the law. Unless that magical day comes when human beings don't do these things, they will continue to cause oil spills.

GLOSSARY

Absorbents—materials used in cleaning spills that soak up oil like a sponge

Bacteria—living organisms that can be seen only by microscope

Ballast—water or other material used to replace cargo so that a ship sails steady in the water

Biodegrade—break down biologically, naturally

Boom—a kind of fence put around an oil slick on water

Burrow—dig in the ground

Carcinogens—cancer-causing agents

Cracking—breaking up petroleum into fractions

Detergents—chemical substitutes for soap

Dispersants—mild detergents

Evaporate—change into a vapor

Food chain—eater-and-eaten patterns

Fractions—products resulting from the distillation of petroleum

Groundwater—water under the ground that feeds springs and wells

Herders—methods of keeping spilled oil from spreading

Hull—the body or structure of a vessel

Hydrocarbons—combinations of hydrogen and carbon

Landspreading—a disposal method for the debris of an oil spill

Mousse—a mixture of water and oil that reaches land in an oil spill

Oil slick—a circular formation of spilled oil

Plankton—microscopic plants and animals that live in the sea

Preens—smoothes; in birds, by using their bills

Pumping—a cleanup method used with skimmers or pumps by themselves

Reefs—ridges of rock, sand, or coral lying at or just under the surface of the water

Refineries—places where petroleum is changed into various products

Residual oils—oils left after distillation or cracking of petroleum

Skimmers—devices to pick up oil off the surface of water

Sorbents. See **Absorbents**

Spawn—to produce many young, especially in fish

Variables—different conditions

Weathering—the action of wind, weather, waves, tides, and sunlight on oil in water

FOR FURTHER READING

Brown, Joseph E. *Oil Spills.* New York: Putnam, 1978.

Fairball, David, and Philip Jordan. *The Wreck of the Amoco Cadiz.* Briarcliff Manor, NY: Scarborough House, 1980.

Hawkes, Nigel. *Oil.* New York: Gloucester, 1985.

Lynch, Michael. *How Oil Rigs are Made.* New York: Facts on File, 1985.

Mitgutsch, Ali. *From Oil to Gasoline.* Minneapolis, MN: Carolrhoda Books, 1981.

Scott, Elaine. *Oil!* New York: Warner, 1984.

Stephen, R. J. *Oil Rigs.* New York: Franklin Watts, 1986.

INDEX

ABOUT THE AUTHOR

Madelyn Klein Anderson is a graduate of Hunter College, New York University, and the Graduate School of Library and Information Science of Pratt Institute, New York. She is a former army officer and occupational therapist who moved into the publishing world and became a senior editor of children's books with a major publishing company before turning to writing full-time.

Ms. Anderson has lived in many areas of the country and has traveled extensively. She now makes her home in New York City.